# Reading Journal

## A COMPLETE READING CURRICULUM FOR GRADES 2-8

## How to Use this Book

This book is designed to supplement your DIY homeschool reading curriculum for elementary grades. For more information on how to create your own curriculum, please enter this web address into your computer's URL bar: bit.ly/1GOr9nJ

The Reading Journal is comprised of 30 lessons to help your child think deeper about the text that he/she is reading. We will cover comprehension, story elements, vocabulary study, compare/contrast, and much more. We will also look at the story in light of God's Word.

This book can be used with any length of text: chapter books or picture books. This will not affect the ability to use the lessons. Each day you will record the title of the book. If you are only reading a portion, simply note the pages read on that day. If you are reading the whole text, it's not necessary to fill that part out.

You may also read fiction or nonfiction. We intentionally designed most pages to fit either type. However there are some that deal with characters and thus wouldn't be a good fit for nonfiction. If you find that a lesson doesn't seem to fit the story, encourage your child to simply skip that one and come back to it later. I tell my children to come back as soon as they start a new text, which is typically the next day when we are reading nonfiction. (Often nonfiction can be read in one day as it doesn't usually contain chapters.)

For your convenience we have duplicated the 30 lessons enough times in this book to cover the entire 180 days of school. If you want less or more, no problem. Simply print those designated pages. The original set is found between pages 4-17, if you would prefer to print only that.

Happy Reading!

*For wisdom will come into your heart, and knowledge will be pleasant to your soul;*
*discretion will watch over you, understanding will guard you.*
*Proverbs 2:10-11*

# Reading Journal

## TEXT TO TEXT

Compare what you have read to another story or text.

| Book Title | |
| --- | --- |
| _____ | |
| _____ | |
| _____ | |
| _____ | |

TEXT #1

_____

SIMILARITIES

TEXT #2

_____

Date:

_____

Pages Read Today:

_____

Rating

☆☆☆☆☆

## KNOW THE TRUTH

Do the facts in this story line up with God's Word?

Book Title

_____

_____

_____

FACT#1_____

_____ ☐ YES   ☐ NO

Biblical support: _____

_____

Date:

_____

FACT#2_____

Pages Read Today:

_____

_____ ☐ YES   ☐ NO

Rating

☆☆☆☆☆

Biblical support: _____

_____

# Reading Journal

Book Title

_____

_____

_____

Date:

_____

Pages Read
Today:

_____

Rating
☆☆☆☆☆

What did you learn in today's reading?

_____

_____

_____

_____

_____

_____

_____

_____

_____

_____

## PURPOSE

Book Title

_____

_____

_____

Date:

_____

Pages Read
Today:

_____

Rating
☆☆☆☆☆

Why do you think the author wrote this book?

☐   To entertain    ☐   To inform

What do you think the author was hoping you would learn?

# Reading Journal

## CHARACTER PROFILE

**Book Title**

_____

_____

_____

_____

**Date:**

_____

**Pages Read Today:**

_____

**Rating**

☆☆☆☆☆

Name: _____ Age: _____ Gender: _____

Likes: _____

_____

Dislikes: _____

_____

Something interesting about this character:

_____

_____

_____

_____

## LIVE IT OUT

**Book Title**

_____

_____

_____

**Date:**

_____

**Pages Read Today:**

_____

**Rating**

☆☆☆☆☆

If you could meet the main character what would you tell him/her about God? Or how would you encourage their faith?

_____

_____

_____

_____

_____

_____

_____

_____

_____

# Reading Journal

## SUPER SLEUTH

Book Title

_____

_____

_____

_____

Date:

_____

Pages Read
Today:

_____

Rating
☆☆☆☆☆

| SETTING | CHARACTERS |
|---|---|
| | |
| PROBLEM | SOLUTION |
| | |

## WISE CHOICES

Book Title

_____

_____

_____

_____

Date:

_____

Pages Read
Today:

_____

Rating
☆☆☆☆☆

List one choice that was made in the story.

_____

_____

Was this choice wise?     ☐   YES     ☐ NO

Defend your answer with a Bible verse.

"

_____

_____

_____

_____
"

_____

_____

# Reading Journal

## WORD STUDY

Pick a word you don't know and define it.

_____

_____

_____

Pick a word and write the synonym and antonym.

SYNONYM

ANTONYM

Pick a word and write three words that rhyme with it.

_____

1. _____

2. _____

3. _____

Book Title

_____

_____

_____

Date:

_____

Pages Read
Today:

_____

Rating
☆☆☆☆☆

## SWITCHAROO

If you could be any character in today's reading who would you be and why?

_____

_____

_____

_____

_____

_____

_____

_____

_____

_____

Book Title

_____

_____

_____

Date:

_____

Pages Read
Today:

_____

Rating
☆☆☆☆☆

# Reading Journal

| Book Title | | | |
|---|---|---|---|
| _____ | | | |
| _____ | | | |
| _____ | | | |
| _____ | | | |
| Date: | | | |
| _____ | | | |
| Pages Read Today: | | | |
| _____ | | | |
| Rating ☆☆☆☆☆ | | | |

## GET INFORMED

Record in each column as you read.

| FACTS | QUESTIONS | RESPONSES |
|---|---|---|
| | | |
| | | |

## THINK ON THESE THINGS

| Book Title |
|---|
| _____ |
| _____ |
| _____ |
| _____ |
| Date: |
| _____ |
| Pages Read Today: |
| _____ |
| Rating ☆☆☆☆☆ |

In Philippians 4:8, the Bible tells us exactly what kinds of things we should think about. Check off the things below that describe this book.

☐ PURE          ☐ LOVELY          ☐ OF GOOD REPORT

☐ VIRTUOUS          ☐ PRAISE-WORTHY

Tell if you would recommend this book and why.

_____

_____

_____

_____

_____

_____

# Reading Journal

**Book Title**

_____

_____

_____

_____

**Date:**

_____

**Pages Read Today:**

_____

**Rating**

☆☆☆☆☆

## IMAGINE IT

Write a different ending to the story.

_____

_____

_____

_____

_____

_____

_____

_____

_____

_____

_____

_____

_____

_____

**Book Title**

_____

_____

_____

_____

**Date:**

_____

**Pages Read Today:**

_____

**Rating**

☆☆☆☆☆

## PURPOSE

Learn more about the time period of this book, the author, or any topic mentioned. Tell what you found.

**FACT#1**

**FACT#2**

**FACT#3**

**FACT#4**

# Reading Journal

## FAVORITES

Book Title

_____

_____

_____

_____

Date:

_____

Pages Read
Today:

_____

Rating

☆☆☆☆☆

What was your favorite part of the story?

_____

_____

_____

_____

_____

_____

_____

_____

_____

_____

_____

## LEARNING TO DISCERN

Book Title

_____

_____

_____

_____

Date:

_____

Pages Read
Today:

_____

Rating

☆☆☆☆☆

What evidence do you find that shows if the character in this story (or the author) would be a good influence on you?

CLUE #2

CLUE #1

# Reading Journal

## B-M-E

| Book Title | | |
|---|---|---|
| _____ | **BEGINNING** | |
| _____ | | |
| _____ | | |
| _____ | **MIDDLE** | |
| Date: | | |
| _____ | | |
| Pages Read Today: | **ENDING** | |
| _____ | | |
| Rating ☆☆☆☆☆ | | |

## INSPIRED

| Book Title | After reading this text, what do you feel inspired to do better? |
|---|---|
| _____ | |
| _____ | |
| _____ | |
| Date: | |
| _____ | |
| Pages Read Today: | |
| _____ | |
| Rating ☆☆☆☆☆ | |

# Reading Journal

## WORD STUDY

Book Title

_____

_____

_____

_____

Date:

_____

Pages Read Today:

_____

Rating
☆☆☆☆☆

Write 3 verbs from today's reading.

1. _____

2. _____

3. _____

Write 3 adjectives from today's reading.

1. _____

2. _____

3. _____

Write 3 nouns from today's reading.

1. _____

2. _____

3. _____

## FACT OR FICTION?

Book Title

_____

_____

_____

_____

Date:

_____

Pages Read Today:

_____

Rating
☆☆☆☆☆

Is this book fact or fiction? Write three clues that help you to know the answer.

Clue#1_____

_____

_____

Clue#2_____

_____

_____

Clue#3_____

_____

_____

The book is ☐ FACT     ☐ FICTION

# Reading Journal

| Book Title | **HAVING COMPASSION** |
|---|---|
| _____ _____ _____ _____ | Have you ever felt like one of the characters in the story?  ☐ YES  ☐ NO |

Have you ever felt like one of the characters in the story?  ☐ YES  ☐ NO

Explain your answer. Then draw about it.

_____

_____

_____

_____

_____

_____

_____

**Book Title**

_____

_____

_____

**Date:**

_____

**Pages Read Today:**

_____

**Rating**

☆☆☆☆☆

## SCENE IT

What was the setting? _____

Draw a scene from the book that wasn't in the pictures.

**Book Title**

_____

_____

_____

**Date:**

_____

**Pages Read Today:**

_____

**Rating**

☆☆☆☆☆

# Reading Journal

©Not Consumed 2016

## SEQUENCE IT

Book Title

_____

_____

_____

Date:

_____

Pages Read
Today:

_____

Rating
☆☆☆☆☆

Write the order of events that happened in the story
or chapter.

First, _____

_____

_____

Next, _____

_____

_____

Last, _____

_____

_____

## DARE TO COMPARE

Book Title

_____

_____

_____

Date:

_____

Pages Read
Today:

_____

Rating
☆☆☆☆☆

Compare yourself with one of the characters.

YOU          BOTH          CHARACTER

# Reading Journal

## SHARE IT

Book Title

_____
_____
_____
_____

Date:
_____

Pages Read Today:
_____

Rating
☆☆☆☆☆

This book is so _____ that I must tell _____ about it.

Here's why:

_____
_____
_____
_____
_____
_____
_____
_____

## I'M WONDERING

Book Title

_____
_____
_____

Date:
_____

Pages Read Today:
_____

Rating
☆☆☆☆☆

Question before reading:

Question while reading:

Question after reading:

# Reading Journal

Book Title

_____
_____
_____
_____

Date:

_____

Pages Read
Today:

_____

Rating

☆☆☆☆☆

## THE BIG IDEA

MAIN
IDEA

DETAIL
#1

DETAIL
#2

Book Title

_____
_____
_____
_____

Date:

_____

Pages Read
Today:

_____

Rating

☆☆☆☆☆

## COMPARE IT TO THE BIBLE

Tell about a Bible verse or passage that comes to mind when you read this story.

_____
_____
_____
_____
_____
_____
_____
_____
_____

# Reading Journal

## TEXT TO TEXT

Compare what you have read to another story or text.

**Book Title**

_____

_____

_____

_____

**Date:**

_____

**Pages Read Today:**

_____

**Rating**
☆☆☆☆☆

TEXT #1

_____

SIMILARITIES

TEXT #2

_____

## KNOW THE TRUTH

Do the facts in this story line up with God's Word?

**Book Title**

_____

_____

_____

_____

**Date:**

_____

**Pages Read Today:**

_____

**Rating**
☆☆☆☆☆

FACT#1_____

_____ ☐ YES  ☐ NO

Biblical support: _____

_____

FACT#2_____

_____ ☐ YES  ☐ NO

Biblical support: _____

_____

# Reading Journal

## LEARN SOMETHING NEW

Book Title

_____

_____

_____

_____

Date:

_____

Pages Read
Today:

_____

Rating

☆☆☆☆☆

What did you learn in today's reading?

_____

_____

_____

_____

_____

_____

_____

_____

_____

_____

## PURPOSE

Book Title

_____

_____

_____

_____

Date:

_____

Pages Read
Today:

_____

Rating

☆☆☆☆☆

Why do you think the author wrote this book?

☐  To entertain    ☐  To inform

What do you think the author was hoping you would learn?

# Reading Journal

## CHARACTER PROFILE

Book Title

_____

_____

_____

_____

Date:

_____

Pages Read Today:

_____

Rating
☆☆☆☆☆

Name: _____ Age: _____ Gender: _____

Likes: _____

_____

Dislikes: _____

_____

Something interesting about this character:

_____

_____

_____

_____

## LIVE IT OUT

Book Title

_____

_____

_____

_____

Date:

_____

Pages Read Today:

_____

Rating
☆☆☆☆☆

If you could meet the main character what would you tell him/her about God? Or how would you encourage their faith?

_____

_____

_____

_____

_____

_____

_____

# Reading Journal

| | |
|---|---|
| Book Title | **SUPER SLEUTH** |

**SETTING**

**CHARACTERS**

**PROBLEM**

**SOLUTION**

Date:

Pages Read Today:

Rating
☆☆☆☆☆

## WISE CHOICES

Book Title

List one choice that was made in the story.

_____

_____

Was this choice wise?　□　YES　□ NO

Defend your answer with a Bible verse.

" _____

_____

_____

_____ "

Date:

Pages Read Today:

Rating
☆☆☆☆☆

_____

# Reading Journal

## WORD STUDY

Book Title

_____

_____

_____

_____

Date:

_____

Pages Read
Today:

_____

Rating
☆☆☆☆☆

Pick a word you don't know and define it.

_____

_____

_____

Pick a word and write the synonym and antonym.

SYNONYM        ANTONYM

Pick a word and write three words that rhyme with it.

_____

1. _____

2. _____

3. _____

## SWITCHAROO

Book Title

_____

_____

_____

_____

Date:

_____

Pages Read
Today:

_____

Rating
☆☆☆☆☆

If you could be any character in today's reading who would you be and why?

_____

_____

_____

_____

_____

_____

_____

_____

_____

# Reading Journal

## GET INFORMED

Record in each column as you read.

**Book Title**

_____

_____

_____

_____

Date:

_____

Pages Read
Today:

_____

Rating
☆☆☆☆☆

| FACTS | QUESTIONS | RESPONSES |
| --- | --- | --- |
|  |  |  |

## THINK ON THESE THINGS

**Book Title**

_____

_____

_____

_____

Date:

_____

Pages Read
Today:

_____

Rating
☆☆☆☆☆

In Philippians 4:8, the Bible tells us exactly what kinds of things we should think about. Check off the things below that describe this book.

☐ PURE ☐ LOVELY ☐ OF GOOD REPORT

☐ VIRTUOUS ☐ PRAISE-WORTHY

Tell if you would recommend this book and why.

_____

_____

_____

_____

_____

_____

# Reading Journal

## IMAGINE IT

**Book Title**

_____
_____
_____
_____

**Date:**

_____

**Pages Read Today:**

_____

**Rating**

☆☆☆☆☆

Write a different ending to the story.

_____
_____
_____
_____
_____
_____
_____
_____
_____
_____
_____
_____
_____
_____

## PURPOSE

**Book Title**

_____
_____
_____
_____

**Date:**

_____

**Pages Read Today:**

_____

**Rating**

☆☆☆☆☆

Learn more about the time period of this book, the author, or any topic mentioned. Tell what you found.

**FACT#1**

**FACT#2**

**FACT#3**

**FACT#4**

# Reading Journal

## FAVORITES

Book Title

_____

_____

_____

Date:

_____

Pages Read Today:

_____

Rating
☆☆☆☆☆

What was your favorite part of the story?

_____

_____

_____

_____

_____

_____

_____

_____

_____

_____

## LEARNING TO DISCERN

Book Title

_____

_____

_____

Date:

_____

Pages Read Today:

_____

Rating
☆☆☆☆☆

What evidence do you find that shows if the character in this story (or the author) would be a good influence on you?

CLUE #1

CLUE #2

# Reading Journal

| | |
|---|---|
| **Book Title** | |
| _____ | |
| _____ | |
| _____ | |
| _____ | |
| **Date:** | |
| _____ | |
| **Pages Read Today:** | |
| _____ | |
| **Rating** ☆☆☆☆☆ | |

## B-M-E

**BEGINNING**

**MIDDLE**

**ENDING**

| | |
|---|---|
| **Book Title** | |
| _____ | |
| _____ | |
| _____ | |
| _____ | |
| **Date:** | |
| _____ | |
| **Pages Read Today:** | |
| _____ | |
| **Rating** ☆☆☆☆☆ | |

## INSPIRED

After reading this text, what do you feel inspired to do better?

_____

_____

_____

_____

_____

_____

_____

_____

_____

_____

# Reading Journal

Book Title

_____

_____

_____

_____

Date:

_____

Pages Read Today:

_____

Rating

☆☆☆☆☆

## WORD STUDY

Write 3 verbs from today's reading.

1. _____

2. _____

3. _____

Write 3 adjectives from today's reading.

1. _____

2. _____

3. _____

Write 3 nouns from today's reading.

1. _____

2. _____

3. _____

---

Book Title

_____

_____

_____

_____

Date:

_____

Pages Read Today:

_____

Rating

☆☆☆☆☆

## FACT OR FICTION?

Is this book fact or fiction? Write three clues that help you to know the answer.

Clue#1_____

_____

_____

Clue#2_____

_____

_____

Clue#3_____

_____

_____

The book is ☐ FACT      ☐ FICTION

# Reading Journal

## HAVING COMPASSION

| Book Title |
| --- |
| _____ |
| _____ |
| _____ |
| _____ |

Date:

_____

Pages Read
Today:

_____

Rating

☆☆☆☆☆

Have you ever felt like one of the characters in the story?     ☐ YES   ☐ NO

Explain your answer. Then draw about it.

_____

_____

_____

_____

_____

_____

_____

_____

_____

## SCENE IT

| Book Title |
| --- |
| _____ |
| _____ |
| _____ |

Date:

_____

Pages Read
Today:

_____

Rating

☆☆☆☆☆

What was the setting? _____

Draw a scene from the book that wasn't in the pictures.

# Reading Journal

## SEQUENCE IT

Book Title

_____
_____
_____

Date:

_____

Pages Read Today:

_____

Rating
☆☆☆☆☆

Write the order of events that happened in the story or chapter.

First, _____

_____

_____

Next, _____

_____

_____

Last, _____

_____

_____

## DARE TO COMPARE

Book Title

_____
_____
_____

Date:

_____

Pages Read Today:

_____

Rating
☆☆☆☆☆

Compare yourself with one of the characters.

YOU          BOTH          CHARACTER

# Reading Journal

## SHARE IT

Book Title

_____

_____

_____

Date:

_____

Pages Read
Today:

_____

Rating
☆☆☆☆☆

This book is so _____ that I must tell _____ about it.

Here's why:

_____

_____

_____

_____

_____

_____

_____

_____

_____

## I'M WONDERING

Book Title

_____

_____

_____

Date:

_____

Pages Read
Today:

_____

Rating
☆☆☆☆☆

Question before reading:

Question while reading:

Question after reading:

# Reading Journal

Book Title

_____
_____
_____
_____

Date:

_____

Pages Read Today:

_____

Rating
☆☆☆☆☆

## THE BIG IDEA

DETAIL #1

MAIN IDEA

DETAIL #2

Book Title

_____
_____
_____
_____

Date:

_____

Pages Read Today:

_____

Rating
☆☆☆☆☆

## COMPARE IT TO THE BIBLE

Tell about a Bible verse or passage that comes to mind when you read this story.

# Reading Journal

## TEXT TO TEXT

**Book Title**

_____
_____
_____
_____

**Date:**

_____

**Pages Read Today:**

_____

**Rating**
☆☆☆☆☆

Compare what you have read to another story or text.

TEXT #1

_____

SIMILARITIES

TEXT #2

_____

## KNOW THE TRUTH

**Book Title**

_____
_____
_____
_____

**Date:**

_____

**Pages Read Today:**

_____

**Rating**
☆☆☆☆☆

Do the facts in this story line up with God's Word?

FACT#1_____
_____

☐ YES    ☐ NO

Biblical support: _____
_____

FACT#2_____
_____

☐ YES    ☐ NO

Biblical support: _____
_____

# Reading Journal

## LEARN SOMETHING NEW

Book Title

_____

_____

_____

Date:

_____

Pages Read Today:

_____

Rating

☆☆☆☆☆

What did you learn in today's reading?

_____

_____

_____

_____

_____

_____

_____

_____

_____

_____

_____

## PURPOSE

Book Title

_____

_____

_____

Date:

_____

Pages Read Today:

_____

Rating

☆☆☆☆☆

Why do you think the author wrote this book?

☐  To entertain      ☐  To inform

What do you think the author was hoping you would learn?

# Reading Journal

## CHARACTER PROFILE

**Book Title**

_____

_____

_____

**Date:**

_____

**Pages Read Today:**

_____

**Rating**
☆☆☆☆☆

Name: _____ Age: _____ Gender: _____

Likes: _____

_____

Dislikes: _____

_____

Something interesting about this character:

_____

_____

_____

_____

_____

## LIVE IT OUT

**Book Title**

_____

_____

_____

**Date:**

_____

**Pages Read Today:**

_____

**Rating**
☆☆☆☆☆

If you could meet the main character what would you tell him/her about God? Or how would you encourage their faith?

_____

_____

_____

_____

_____

_____

_____

_____

# Reading Journal

| Book Title | SUPER SLEUTH | |
|---|---|---|
| _____ | SETTING | CHARACTERS |
| _____ | | |
| _____ | | |
| _____ | | |
| Date: | | |
| _____ | PROBLEM | SOLUTION |
| Pages Read Today: | | |
| _____ | | |
| Rating ☆☆☆☆☆ | | |

**WISE CHOICES**

Book Title

_____
_____
_____
_____

Date:

_____

Pages Read Today:

_____

Rating
☆☆☆☆☆

List one choice that was made in the story.

_____

_____

Was this choice wise?    ☐ YES    ☐ NO

Defend your answer with a Bible verse.

"
_____
_____
_____
_____ "
_____

_____

# Reading Journal

## WORD STUDY

Pick a word you don't know and define it.

_____

_____

Pick a word and write the synonym and antonym.

SYNONYM

ANTONYM

Pick a word and write three words that rhyme with it.

_____

1. _____

2. _____

3. _____

Book Title

_____

_____

_____

Date:

_____

Pages Read Today:

_____

Rating
☆☆☆☆☆

## SWITCHAROO

If you could be any character in today's reading who would you be and why?

_____

_____

_____

_____

_____

_____

_____

_____

Book Title

_____

_____

_____

Date:

_____

Pages Read Today:

_____

Rating
☆☆☆☆☆

# Reading Journal

## GET INFORMED

| Book Title | Record in each column as you read. | | |
|---|---|---|---|
| _____ | FACTS | QUESTIONS | RESPONSES |
| _____ | | | |
| _____ | | | |
| _____ | | | |
| Date: | | | |
| _____ | | | |
| Pages Read Today: | | | |
| _____ | | | |
| Rating ☆☆☆☆☆ | | | |

## THINK ON THESE THINGS

**Book Title**

_____

_____

_____

_____

**Date:**

_____

**Pages Read Today:**

_____

**Rating**
☆☆☆☆☆

In Philippians 4:8, the Bible tells us exactly what kinds of things we should think about. Check off the things below that describe this book.

☐ PURE ☐ LOVELY ☐ OF GOOD REPORT

☐ VIRTUOUS ☐ PRAISE-WORTHY

Tell if you would recommend this book and why.

_____

_____

_____

_____

_____

# Reading Journal

## IMAGINE IT

**Book Title**

_____
_____
_____

**Date:**

_____

**Pages Read Today:**

_____

**Rating**
☆☆☆☆☆

Write a different ending to the story.

_____
_____
_____
_____
_____
_____
_____
_____
_____
_____
_____

## PURPOSE

**Book Title**

_____
_____
_____

**Date:**

_____

**Pages Read Today:**

_____

**Rating**
☆☆☆☆☆

Learn more about the time period of this book, the author, or any topic mentioned. Tell what you found.

FACT#1

FACT#2

FACT#3

FACT#4

# Reading Journal

## FAVORITES

Book Title

_____

_____

_____

_____

Date:

_____

Pages Read Today:

_____

Rating
☆☆☆☆☆

What was your favorite part of the story?

## LEARNING TO DISCERN

Book Title

_____

_____

_____

_____

Date:

_____

Pages Read Today:

_____

Rating
☆☆☆☆☆

What evidence do you find that shows if the character in this story (or the author) would be a good influence on you?

CLUE#1

CLUE#2

# Reading Journal

**Book Title**

_____

_____

_____

**Date:**

_____

**Pages Read Today:**

_____

**Rating**
☆☆☆☆☆

## B-M-E

| BEGINNING | |
|---|---|
| MIDDLE | |
| ENDING | |

**Book Title**

_____

_____

_____

_____

**Date:**

_____

**Pages Read Today:**

_____

**Rating**
☆☆☆☆☆

## INSPIRED

After reading this text, what do you feel inspired to do better?

_____

_____

_____

_____

_____

_____

_____

_____

_____

_____

# Reading Journal

## WORD STUDY

**Book Title**

_____

_____

_____

**Date:**

_____

**Pages Read Today:**

_____

**Rating**
☆☆☆☆☆

| Write 3 verbs from today's reading. | Write 3 adjectives from today's reading. | Write 3 nouns from today's reading. |
|---|---|---|
| 1. _____ | 1. _____ | 1. _____ |
| 2. _____ | 2. _____ | 2. _____ |
| 3. _____ | 3. _____ | 3. _____ |

## FACT OR FICTION?

**Book Title**

_____

_____

_____

**Date:**

_____

**Pages Read Today:**

_____

**Rating**
☆☆☆☆☆

Is this book fact or fiction? Write three clues that help you to know the answer.

Clue#1_____

_____

_____

Clue#2_____

_____

_____

Clue#3_____

_____

_____

The book is ☐ FACT      ☐ FICTION

# Reading Journal

## HAVING COMPASSION

Book Title

_____

_____

_____

_____

Date:

_____

Pages Read
Today:

_____

Rating

☆☆☆☆☆

Have you ever felt like one of the characters in the story?  ☐ YES  ☐ NO

Explain your answer. Then draw about it.

_____

_____

_____

_____

_____

_____

_____

_____

_____

## SCENE IT

Book Title

_____

_____

_____

Date:

_____

Pages Read
Today:

_____

Rating

☆☆☆☆☆

What was the setting? _____
Draw a scene from the book that wasn't in the pictures.

# Reading Journal

## SEQUENCE IT

**Book Title**

_____

_____

_____

_____

**Date:**

_____

**Pages Read Today:**

_____

**Rating**

☆☆☆☆☆

Write the order of events that happened in the story or chapter.

First, _____

_____

_____

Next, _____

_____

_____

Last, _____

_____

_____

## DARE TO COMPARE

**Book Title**

_____

_____

_____

_____

**Date:**

_____

**Pages Read Today:**

_____

**Rating**

☆☆☆☆☆

Compare yourself with one of the characters.

YOU          BOTH          CHARACTER

# Reading Journal

## SHARE IT

**Book Title**

_____

_____

_____

**Date:**

_____

**Pages Read Today:**

_____

**Rating**

☆☆☆☆☆

This book is so _____ that I must tell _____ about it.

Here's why:

_____

_____

_____

_____

_____

_____

_____

_____

## I'M WONDERING

**Book Title**

_____

_____

_____

**Date:**

_____

**Pages Read Today:**

_____

**Rating**

☆☆☆☆☆

Question before reading:

Question while reading:

Question after reading:

# Reading Journal

Book Title

_____

_____

_____

_____

Date:

_____

Pages Read Today:

_____

Rating

☆☆☆☆☆

## THE BIG IDEA

DETAIL #1

MAIN IDEA

DETAIL #2

Book Title

_____

_____

_____

_____

Date:

_____

Pages Read Today:

_____

Rating

☆☆☆☆☆

## COMPARE IT TO THE BIBLE

Tell about a Bible verse or passage that comes to mind when you read this story.

_____

_____

_____

_____

_____

_____

_____

_____

_____

_____

_____

# Reading Journal

## TEXT TO TEXT

Compare what you have read to another story or text.

TEXT #1 _____

SIMILARITIES

TEXT #2 _____

**Book Title**

_____

_____

_____

**Date:**

_____

**Pages Read Today:**

_____

**Rating**

☆☆☆☆☆

## KNOW THE TRUTH

Do the facts in this story line up with God's Word?

FACT#1_____

_____ ☐ YES ☐ NO

Biblical support: _____

_____

FACT#2_____

_____ ☐ YES ☐ NO

Biblical support: _____

_____

**Book Title**

_____

_____

_____

_____

**Date:**

_____

**Pages Read Today:**

_____

**Rating**

☆☆☆☆☆

# Reading Journal

## LEARN SOMETHING NEW

Book Title

_____
_____
_____
_____

Date:

_____

Pages Read
Today:

_____

Rating
☆☆☆☆☆

What did you learn in today's reading?

_____
_____
_____
_____
_____
_____
_____
_____
_____
_____
_____
_____

## PURPOSE

Book Title

_____
_____
_____

Date:

_____

Pages Read
Today:

_____

Rating
☆☆☆☆☆

Why do you think the author wrote this book?

☐  To entertain  ☐  To inform

What do you think the author was hoping you would learn?

# Reading Journal

## CHARACTER PROFILE

Book Title

_____

_____

_____

Date:

_____

Pages Read
Today:

_____

Rating
☆☆☆☆☆

Name: _____ Age: _____ Gender: _____

Likes: _____

_____

Dislikes: _____

_____

Something interesting about this character:

_____

_____

_____

_____

## LIVE IT OUT

Book Title

_____

_____

_____

Date:

_____

Pages Read
Today:

_____

Rating
☆☆☆☆☆

If you could meet the main character what would you tell him/her about God? Or how would you encourage their faith?

_____

_____

_____

_____

_____

_____

 Reading Journal

## SUPER SLEUTH

| Book Title | SETTING | CHARACTERS |
| --- | --- | --- |
| _____ | | |
| _____ | | |
| _____ | | |
| _____ | | |
| Date: | | |
| _____ | PROBLEM | SOLUTION |
| Pages Read Today: | | |
| _____ | | |
| Rating ☆☆☆☆☆ | | |

## WISE CHOICES

Book Title

_____

_____

_____

List one choice that was made in the story.

_____

_____

Was this choice wise?　☐　YES　☐ NO

Date:

_____

Defend your answer with a Bible verse.

"

Pages Read Today:

_____

Rating ☆☆☆☆☆

_____

_____

_____

"

_____

_____

# Reading Journal

## WORD STUDY

Book Title

_____

_____

_____

Date:

_____

Pages Read Today:

_____

Rating
☆☆☆☆☆

Pick a word you don't know and define it.

_____

_____

Pick a word and write the synonym and antonym.

SYNONYM

ANTONYM

Pick a word and write three words that rhyme with it.

_____

1. _____

2. _____

3. _____

## SWITCHAROO

Book Title

_____

_____

_____

Date:

_____

Pages Read Today:

_____

Rating
☆☆☆☆☆

If you could be any character in today's reading who would you be and why?

_____

_____

_____

_____

_____

_____

_____

_____

_____

_____

_____

# Reading Journal

## GET INFORMED

| Book Title | Record in each column as you read. | | |
|---|---|---|---|
| _____ | **FACTS** | **QUESTIONS** | **RESPONSES** |
| _____ | | | |
| _____ | | | |
| _____ | | | |
| Date: | | | |
| _____ | | | |
| Pages Read Today: | | | |
| _____ | | | |
| Rating ☆☆☆☆☆ | | | |

## THINK ON THESE THINGS

**Book Title**

_____

_____

_____

_____

**Date:**

_____

**Pages Read Today:**

_____

**Rating**
☆☆☆☆☆

In Philippians 4:8, the Bible tells us exactly what kinds of things we should think about. Check off the things below that describe this book.

☐ PURE          ☐ LOVELY          ☐ OF GOOD REPORT

☐ VIRTUOUS          ☐ PRAISE-WORTHY

Tell if you would recommend this book and why.

_____

_____

_____

_____

_____

_____

# Reading Journal

## IMAGINE IT

Book Title

_____

_____

Date:

_____

Pages Read Today:

_____

Rating

☆☆☆☆☆

Write a different ending to the story.

_____
_____
_____
_____
_____
_____
_____
_____
_____
_____
_____

## PURPOSE

Book Title

_____

_____

_____

Date:

_____

Pages Read Today:

_____

Rating

☆☆☆☆☆

Learn more about the time period of this book, the author, or any topic mentioned. Tell what you found.

FACT#1

FACT#2

FACT#3

FACT#4

# Reading Journal

## FAVORITES

**Book Title**

_____

_____

_____

**Date:**

_____

**Pages Read Today:**

_____

**Rating**
☆☆☆☆☆

What was your favorite part of the story?

_____

_____

_____

_____

_____

_____

_____

_____

_____

_____

_____

## LEARNING TO DISCERN

**Book Title**

_____

_____

_____

**Date:**

_____

**Pages Read Today:**

_____

**Rating**
☆☆☆☆☆

What evidence do you find that shows if the character in this story (or the author) would be a good influence on you?

CLUE#1

CLUE#2

# Reading Journal

| | B-M-E |
|---|---|
| **Book Title** _____ _____ _____ | |
| | BEGINNING |
| **Date:** _____ | MIDDLE |
| **Pages Read Today:** _____ | |
| **Rating** ☆☆☆☆☆ | ENDING |

## INSPIRED

**Book Title**
_____
_____
_____

**Date:**
_____

**Pages Read Today:**
_____

**Rating**
☆☆☆☆☆

After reading this text, what do you feel inspired to do better?

_____
_____
_____
_____
_____
_____
_____
_____

# Reading Journal

## WORD STUDY

Book Title

_____

_____

_____

_____

Date:

_____

Pages Read
Today:

_____

Rating
☆☆☆☆☆

Write 3 verbs from today's reading.

1. _____

2. _____

3. _____

Write 3 adjectives from today's reading.

1. _____

2. _____

3. _____

Write 3 nouns from today's reading.

1. _____

2. _____

3. _____

## FACT OR FICTION?

Book Title

_____

_____

_____

_____

Date:

_____

Pages Read
Today:

_____

Rating
☆☆☆☆☆

Is this book fact or fiction? Write three clues that help you to know the answer.

Clue#1 _____

_____

_____

Clue#2 _____

_____

Clue#3 _____

_____

_____

The book is ☐ FACT        ☐ FICTION

# Reading Journal

## HAVING COMPASSION

| Book Title |
| --- |
| _____ |
| _____ |
| _____ |
| _____ |

**Date:**
_____

**Pages Read Today:**
_____

**Rating**
☆☆☆☆☆

Have you ever felt like one of the characters in the story?　☐ YES　☐ NO

Explain your answer. Then draw about it.

_____

_____

_____

_____

_____

_____

_____

_____

## SCENE IT

| Book Title |
| --- |
| _____ |
| _____ |
| _____ |
| _____ |

**Date:**
_____

**Pages Read Today:**
_____

**Rating**
☆☆☆☆☆

What was the setting? _____

Draw a scene from the book that wasn't in the pictures.

# Reading Journal

## Book Title

_____

_____

_____

_____

## Date:

_____

## Pages Read Today:

_____

## Rating

☆☆☆☆☆

---

## SEQUENCE IT

Write the order of events that happened in the story or chapter.

First, _____

_____

_____

Next, _____

_____

_____

Last, _____

_____

_____

---

## DARE TO COMPARE

## Book Title

_____

_____

_____

_____

## Date:

_____

## Pages Read Today:

_____

## Rating

☆☆☆☆☆

Compare yourself with one of the characters.

YOU    BOTH    CHARACTER

# Reading Journal

## SHARE IT

Book Title

_____

_____

_____

_____

Date:

_____

Pages Read Today:

_____

Rating

☆☆☆☆☆

This book is so _____ that I must tell _____ about it.

Here's why:

_____

_____

_____

_____

_____

_____

_____

_____

_____

_____

_____

## I'M WONDERING

Book Title

_____

_____

_____

_____

Date:

_____

Pages Read Today:

_____

Rating

☆☆☆☆☆

Question before reading:

Question while reading:

Question after reading:

# Reading Journal

## THE BIG IDEA

Book Title

_____

_____

_____

_____

Date:

_____

Pages Read
Today:

_____

Rating

☆☆☆☆☆

MAIN
IDEA

DETAIL
#1

DETAIL
#2

## COMPARE IT TO THE BIBLE

Book Title

_____

_____

_____

_____

Date:

_____

Pages Read
Today:

_____

Rating

☆☆☆☆☆

Tell about a Bible verse or passage that comes to mind when you read this story.

_____

_____

_____

_____

_____

_____

_____

_____

_____

# Reading Journal

## TEXT TO TEXT

Compare what you have read to another story or text.

**Book Title**

_____

_____

_____

_____

**Date:**

_____

**Pages Read Today:**

_____

**Rating**

☆☆☆☆☆

TEXT #1

_____

SIMILARITIES

TEXT #2

_____

## KNOW THE TRUTH

Do the facts in this story line up with God's Word?

**Book Title**

_____

_____

_____

_____

**Date:**

_____

**Pages Read Today:**

_____

**Rating**

☆☆☆☆☆

FACT#1_____

_____  ☐ YES   ☐ NO

Biblical support: _____

_____

FACT#2_____

_____  ☐ YES   ☐ NO

Biblical support: _____

_____

# Reading Journal

## LEARN SOMETHING NEW

Book Title

_____
_____
_____
_____

Date:

_____

Pages Read Today:

_____

Rating
☆☆☆☆☆

What did you learn in today's reading?

_____
_____
_____
_____
_____
_____
_____
_____
_____
_____
_____

## PURPOSE

Book Title

_____
_____
_____
_____

Date:

_____

Pages Read Today:

_____

Rating
☆☆☆☆☆

Why do you think the author wrote this book?

☐ To entertain   ☐ To inform

What do you think the author was hoping you would learn?

# Reading Journal

## CHARACTER PROFILE

**Book Title**

_____
_____
_____
_____

**Date:**

_____

**Pages Read Today:**

_____

**Rating**
☆☆☆☆☆

Name: _____ Age: _____ Gender: _____

Likes: _____

_____

Dislikes: _____

_____

Something interesting about this character:

_____

_____

_____

_____

_____

## LIVE IT OUT

**Book Title**

_____
_____
_____
_____

**Date:**

_____

**Pages Read Today:**

_____

**Rating**
☆☆☆☆☆

If you could meet the main character what would you tell him/her about God? Or how would you encourage their faith?

_____

_____

_____

_____

_____

_____

_____

_____

# Reading Journal

## SUPER SLEUTH

Book Title

_____
_____
_____
_____

Date:

_____

Pages Read
Today:

_____

Rating
☆☆☆☆☆

| SETTING | CHARACTERS |
|---|---|
| PROBLEM | SOLUTION |

## WISE CHOICES

Book Title

_____
_____
_____
_____

Date:

_____

Pages Read
Today:

_____

Rating
☆☆☆☆☆

List one choice that was made in the story.

_____

_____

Was this choice wise?   ☐ YES   ☐ NO

Defend your answer with a Bible verse.

"
_____
_____
_____
_____ "

_____

# Reading Journal

## WORD STUDY

**Book Title**

_____

_____

_____

_____

**Date:**

_____

**Pages Read Today:**

_____

**Rating**
☆☆☆☆☆

Pick a word you don't know and define it.

_____

_____

Pick a word and write the synonym and antonym.

SYNONYM

ANTONYM

Pick a word and write three words that rhyme with it.

_____

1. _____

2. _____

3. _____

## SWITCHAROO

**Book Title**

_____

_____

_____

_____

**Date:**

_____

**Pages Read Today:**

_____

**Rating**
☆☆☆☆☆

If you could be any character in today's reading who would you be and why?

_____

_____

_____

_____

_____

_____

_____

_____

_____

_____

# Reading Journal

| Book Title | GET INFORMED |
|---|---|
| _____ _____ _____ _____ **Date:** _____ **Pages Read Today:** _____ **Rating** ☆☆☆☆☆ | Record in each column as you read. |

| FACTS | QUESTIONS | RESPONSES |
|---|---|---|
| | | |

## THINK ON THESE THINGS

| Book Title | |
|---|---|
| _____ _____ _____ _____ **Date:** _____ **Pages Read Today:** _____ **Rating** ☆☆☆☆☆ | In Philippians 4:8, the Bible tells us exactly what kinds of things we should think about. Check off the things below that describe this book. |

☐ PURE   ☐ LOVELY   ☐ OF GOOD REPORT

☐ VIRTUOUS   ☐ PRAISE-WORTHY

Tell if you would recommend this book and why.

_____

_____

_____

_____

_____

_____

# Reading Journal

## IMAGINE IT

Book Title

_____
_____
_____
_____

Date:

_____

Pages Read
Today:

_____

Rating
☆☆☆☆☆

Write a different ending to the story.

_____
_____
_____
_____
_____
_____
_____
_____
_____
_____
_____

## PURPOSE

Book Title

_____
_____
_____

Date:

_____

Pages Read
Today:

_____

Rating
☆☆☆☆☆

Learn more about the time period of this book, the author, or any topic mentioned.
Tell what you found.

FACT#1

FACT#2

FACT#3

FACT#4

# Reading Journal

## FAVORITES

Book Title

_____
_____
_____
_____

Date:
_____

Pages Read
Today:
_____

Rating
☆☆☆☆☆

What was your favorite part of the story?

_____
_____
_____
_____
_____
_____
_____
_____
_____
_____
_____

## LEARNING TO DISCERN

Book Title

_____
_____
_____
_____

Date:
_____

Pages Read
Today:
_____

Rating
☆☆☆☆☆

What evidence do you find that shows if the character in this story (or the author) would be a good influence on you?

CLUE #2

CLUE #1

# Reading Journal

## B-M-E

| | |
|---|---|
| Book Title<br><br>_____<br>_____<br>_____<br><br>Date:<br><br>_____<br><br>Pages Read Today:<br><br>_____<br><br>Rating<br>☆☆☆☆☆ | **BEGINNING** |
| | **MIDDLE** |
| | **ENDING** |

## INSPIRED

After reading this text, what do you feel inspired to do better?

| | |
|---|---|
| Book Title<br><br>_____<br>_____<br>_____<br><br>Date:<br><br>_____<br><br>Pages Read Today:<br><br>_____<br><br>Rating<br>☆☆☆☆☆ | _____<br>_____<br>_____<br>_____<br>_____<br>_____<br>_____<br>_____<br>_____ |

# Reading Journal

## WORD STUDY

| Book Title | Write 3 verbs from today's reading. | Write 3 adjectives from today's reading. | Write 3 nouns from today's reading. |
|---|---|---|---|
| _____ | 1. _____ | 1. _____ | 1. _____ |
| _____ | 2. _____ | 2. _____ | 2. _____ |
| _____ | 3. _____ | 3. _____ | 3. _____ |

**Date:**

_____

**Pages Read Today:**

_____

**Rating**
☆☆☆☆☆

## FACT OR FICTION?

Book Title

_____

_____

_____

_____

**Date:**

_____

**Pages Read Today:**

_____

**Rating**
☆☆☆☆☆

Is this book fact or fiction? Write three clues that help you to know the answer.

Clue#1 _____

_____

_____

Clue#2 _____

_____

_____

Clue#3 _____

_____

_____

The book is ☐ FACT ☐ FICTION

# Reading Journal

## HAVING COMPASSION

Book Title

_____

_____

_____

Date:

_____

Pages Read
Today:

_____

Rating
☆☆☆☆☆

Have you ever felt like one of the characters in the story?  ☐ YES  ☐ NO

Explain your answer. Then draw about it.

_____

_____

_____

_____

_____

_____

_____

_____

_____

_____

## SCENE IT

Book Title

_____

_____

_____

Date:

_____

Pages Read
Today:

_____

Rating
☆☆☆☆☆

What was the setting? _____

Draw a scene from the book that wasn't in the pictures.

# Reading Journal

## SEQUENCE IT

**Book Title**

_____

_____

_____

_____

**Date:**

_____

**Pages Read Today:**

_____

**Rating**
☆☆☆☆☆

Write the order of events that happened in the story or chapter.

First, _____

_____

_____

Next, _____

_____

_____

Last, _____

_____

_____

## DARE TO COMPARE

**Book Title**

_____

_____

_____

_____

**Date:**

_____

**Pages Read Today:**

_____

**Rating**
☆☆☆☆☆

Compare yourself with one of the characters.

YOU    BOTH    CHARACTER

# Reading Journal

## SHARE IT

Book Title

_____
_____
_____
_____

Date:

_____

Pages Read Today:

_____

Rating
☆☆☆☆☆

This book is so _____ that I must tell _____ about it.

Here's why:

_____
_____
_____
_____
_____
_____
_____
_____
_____
_____

## I'M WONDERING

Book Title

_____
_____
_____
_____

Date:

_____

Pages Read Today:

_____

Rating
☆☆☆☆☆

Question before reading:

Question while reading:

Question after reading:

# Reading Journal

## THE BIG IDEA

Book Title

_____

_____

_____

Date:

_____

Pages Read
Today:

_____

Rating
☆☆☆☆☆

DETAIL #1

MAIN IDEA

DETAIL #2

## COMPARE IT TO THE BIBLE

Book Title

_____

_____

_____

Date:

_____

Pages Read
Today:

_____

Rating
☆☆☆☆☆

Tell about a Bible verse or passage that comes to mind when you read this story.

_____

_____

_____

_____

_____

_____

_____

_____

_____

# Reading Journal

## TEXT TO TEXT

**Book Title**

_____

_____

_____

**Date:**

_____

**Pages Read Today:**

_____

**Rating**
☆☆☆☆☆

Compare what you have read to another story or text.

TEXT #1

_____

SIMILARITIES

TEXT #2

_____

## KNOW THE TRUTH

**Book Title**

_____

_____

_____

**Date:**

_____

**Pages Read Today:**

_____

**Rating**
☆☆☆☆☆

Do the facts in this story line up with God's Word?

FACT#1_____

_____ ☐ YES  ☐ NO

Biblical support: _____

_____

FACT#2_____

_____ ☐ YES  ☐ NO

Biblical support: _____

_____

# Reading Journal

## LEARN SOMETHING NEW

Book Title

_____
_____
_____
_____

Date:

_____

Pages Read
Today:

_____

Rating
☆☆☆☆☆

What did you learn in today's reading?

_____
_____
_____
_____
_____
_____
_____
_____
_____
_____
_____
_____

## PURPOSE

Book Title

_____
_____
_____
_____

Date:

_____

Pages Read
Today:

_____

Rating
☆☆☆☆☆

Why do you think the author wrote this book?

☐   To entertain   ☐   To inform

What do you think the author was hoping you would learn?

# Reading Journal

## CHARACTER PROFILE

**Book Title**

_____

_____

_____

_____

**Date:**

_____

**Pages Read Today:**

_____

**Rating**
☆☆☆☆☆

Name: _____ Age: _____ Gender: _____

Likes: _____

_____

Dislikes: _____

_____

Something interesting about this character:

_____

_____

_____

_____

## LIVE IT OUT

**Book Title**

_____

_____

_____

_____

**Date:**

_____

**Pages Read Today:**

_____

**Rating**
☆☆☆☆☆

If you could meet the main character what would you tell him/her about God? Or how would you encourage their faith?

_____

_____

_____

_____

_____

_____

_____

# Reading Journal

## SUPER SLEUTH

Book Title

_____

_____

_____

_____

Date:

_____

Pages Read
Today:

_____

Rating
☆☆☆☆☆

| SETTING | CHARACTERS |
|---------|------------|
| | |
| **PROBLEM** | **SOLUTION** |
| | |

## WISE CHOICES

Book Title

_____

_____

_____

_____

Date:

_____

Pages Read
Today:

_____

Rating
☆☆☆☆☆

List one choice that was made in the story.

_____

_____

Was this choice wise?     ☐   YES     ☐ NO

Defend your answer with a Bible verse.

"

_____

_____

_____

_____ "

_____

# Reading Journal

## WORD STUDY

Book Title

_____

_____

_____

_____

Date:

_____

Pages Read
Today:

_____

Rating
☆☆☆☆☆

Pick a word you don't know and define it.

_____

_____

Pick a word and write the synonym and antonym.

SYNONYM

ANTONYM

Pick a word and write three words that rhyme with it.

_____

1. _____

2. _____

3. _____

## SWITCHAROO

Book Title

_____

_____

_____

_____

Date:

_____

Pages Read
Today:

_____

Rating
☆☆☆☆☆

If you could be any character in today's reading who would you be and why?

_____

_____

_____

_____

_____

_____

_____

_____

_____

# Reading Journal

## GET INFORMED

| Book Title | Record in each column as you read. | | |
|---|---|---|---|
| _____ | FACTS | QUESTIONS | RESPONSES |
| _____ | | | |
| _____ | | | |
| _____ | | | |
| Date: _____ | | | |
| _____ | | | |
| Pages Read Today: _____ | | | |
| Rating ☆☆☆☆☆ | | | |

## THINK ON THESE THINGS

**Book Title**

_____

_____

_____

_____

**Date:**

_____

**Pages Read Today:**

_____

**Rating**

☆☆☆☆☆

In Philippians 4:8, the Bible tells us exactly what kinds of things we should think about. Check off the things below that describe this book.

☐ PURE ☐ LOVELY ☐ OF GOOD REPORT

☐ VIRTUOUS ☐ PRAISE-WORTHY

Tell if you would recommend this book and why.

_____

_____

_____

_____

_____

_____

# Reading Journal

## IMAGINE IT

Book Title

_____

_____

_____

Date:

_____

Pages Read Today:

_____

Rating
☆☆☆☆☆

Write a different ending to the story.

_____
_____
_____
_____
_____
_____
_____
_____
_____
_____
_____
_____
_____
_____

## PURPOSE

Book Title

_____

_____

_____

Date:

_____

Pages Read Today:

_____

Rating
☆☆☆☆☆

Learn more about the time period of this book, the author, or any topic mentioned. Tell what you found.

FACT#1

FACT#2

FACT#3

FACT#4

# Reading Journal

## FAVORITES

**Book Title**

_____
_____
_____

**Date:**

_____

**Pages Read Today:**

_____

**Rating**
☆☆☆☆☆

What was your favorite part of the story?

_____
_____
_____
_____
_____
_____
_____
_____
_____
_____
_____
_____

## LEARNING TO DISCERN

**Book Title**

_____
_____
_____

**Date:**

_____

**Pages Read Today:**

_____

**Rating**
☆☆☆☆☆

What evidence do you find that shows if the character in this story (or the author) would be a good influence on you?

CLUE#1

CLUE#2

# Reading Journal

## B-M-E

| | |
|---|---|
| **Book Title** | |
| _____ | |
| _____ | BEGINNING |
| _____ | |
| _____ | |
| **Date:** | MIDDLE |
| _____ | |
| **Pages Read Today:** | |
| _____ | ENDING |
| **Rating** ☆☆☆☆☆ | |

## INSPIRED

| | |
|---|---|
| **Book Title** | After reading this text, what do you feel inspired to do better? |
| _____ | |
| _____ | _____ |
| _____ | _____ |
| _____ | _____ |
| **Date:** | _____ |
| _____ | _____ |
| **Pages Read Today:** | _____ |
| _____ | _____ |
| **Rating** ☆☆☆☆☆ | _____ |

# Reading Journal

## WORD STUDY

| Book Title | Write 3 verbs from today's reading. | Write 3 adjectives from today's reading. | Write 3 nouns from today's reading. |
|---|---|---|---|

_____

_____

_____

Date:

_____

Pages Read Today:

_____

Rating

☆☆☆☆☆

**Write 3 verbs from today's reading.**

1. _____

2. _____

3. _____

**Write 3 adjectives from today's reading.**

1. _____

2. _____

3. _____

**Write 3 nouns from today's reading.**

1. _____

2. _____

3. _____

## FACT OR FICTION?

Book Title

_____

_____

_____

Date:

_____

Pages Read Today:

_____

Rating

☆☆☆☆☆

Is this book fact or fiction? Write three clues that help you to know the answer.

Clue#1_____

_____

_____

Clue#2_____

_____

_____

Clue#3_____

_____

_____

The book is ☐ FACT ☐ FICTION

# Reading Journal

## HAVING COMPASSION

| Book Title |
| --- |
| _____ |
| _____ |
| _____ |
| _____ |

Date:

_____

Pages Read
Today:

_____

Rating

☆☆☆☆☆

Have you ever felt like one of the characters in the story?  □ YES  □ NO

Explain your answer. Then draw about it.

_____

_____

_____

_____

_____

_____

_____

_____

_____

## SCENE IT

| Book Title |
| --- |
| _____ |
| _____ |
| _____ |
| _____ |

Date:

_____

Pages Read
Today:

_____

Rating

☆☆☆☆☆

What was the setting? _____
Draw a scene from the book that wasn't in the pictures.

# Reading Journal

## SEQUENCE IT

| Book Title |
| --- |
| _____ |
| _____ |
| _____ |
| _____ |

Date:
_____

Pages Read Today:
_____

Rating
☆☆☆☆☆

Write the order of events that happened in the story or chapter.

First, _____

_____

_____

Next, _____

_____

_____

Last, _____

_____

## DARE TO COMPARE

| Book Title |
| --- |
| _____ |
| _____ |
| _____ |
| _____ |

Date:
_____

Pages Read Today:
_____

Rating
☆☆☆☆☆

Compare yourself with one of the characters.

YOU        BOTH        CHARACTER

# Reading Journal

## SHARE IT

Book Title

_____

_____

_____

_____

Date:

_____

Pages Read
Today:

_____

Rating
☆☆☆☆☆

This book is so _____ that I must tell _____ about it.

Here's why:

_____

_____

_____

_____

_____

_____

_____

_____

_____

## I'M WONDERING

Book Title

_____

_____

_____

_____

Date:

_____

Pages Read
Today:

_____

Rating
☆☆☆☆☆

Question before reading:

Question while reading:

Question after reading:

# Reading Journal

## THE BIG IDEA

Book Title

_____

_____

_____

_____

Date:

_____

Pages Read
Today:

_____

Rating
☆☆☆☆☆

MAIN
IDEA

DETAIL
#1

DETAIL
#2

## COMPARE IT TO THE BIBLE

Book Title

_____

_____

_____

_____

Date:

_____

Pages Read
Today:

_____

Rating
☆☆☆☆☆

Tell about a Bible verse or passage that comes to mind when you read this story.

_____

_____

_____

_____

_____

_____

_____

_____

_____

_____

# Reading Journal

## TEXT TO TEXT

Book Title

_____

_____

_____

_____

Date:

_____

Pages Read
Today:

_____

Rating

☆☆☆☆☆

Compare what you have read to another story or text.

TEXT #1

_____

SIMILARITIES

TEXT #2

_____

## KNOW THE TRUTH

Book Title

_____

_____

_____

_____

Date:

_____

Pages Read
Today:

_____

Rating

☆☆☆☆☆

Do the facts in this story line up with God's Word?

FACT#1 _____

_____  ☐ YES   ☐ NO

Biblical support: _____

_____

FACT#2 _____

_____  ☐ YES   ☐ NO

Biblical support: _____

_____

# Reading Journal

## LEARN SOMETHING NEW

Book Title

_____
_____
_____
_____

Date:

_____

Pages Read Today:

_____

Rating
☆☆☆☆☆

What did you learn in today's reading?

_____
_____
_____
_____
_____
_____
_____
_____
_____
_____
_____
_____

## PURPOSE

Book Title

_____
_____
_____

Date:

_____

Pages Read Today:

_____

Rating
☆☆☆☆☆

Why do you think the author wrote this book?

☐ To entertain   ☐ To inform

What do you think the author was hoping you would learn?

# Reading Journal

## CHARACTER PROFILE

**Book Title**

_____

_____

_____

_____

**Date:**

_____

**Pages Read Today:**

_____

**Rating**
☆☆☆☆☆

Name: _____ Age: _____ Gender: _____

Likes: _____

_____

Dislikes: _____

_____

Something interesting about this character:

_____

_____

_____

_____

## LIVE IT OUT

**Book Title**

_____

_____

_____

_____

**Date:**

_____

**Pages Read Today:**

_____

**Rating**
☆☆☆☆☆

If you could meet the main character what would you tell him/her about God? Or how would you encourage their faith?

_____

_____

_____

_____

_____

_____

_____

_____

# Reading Journal

| Book Title | SUPER SLEUTH | |
|---|---|---|
| _____ | **SETTING** | **CHARACTERS** |
| _____ | | |
| _____ | | |
| **Date:** | | |
| _____ | **PROBLEM** | **SOLUTION** |
| **Pages Read Today:** | | |
| _____ | | |
| **Rating** ☆☆☆☆☆ | | |

## WISE CHOICES

**Book Title**

_____

_____

_____

_____

**Date:**

_____

**Pages Read Today:**

_____

**Rating** ☆☆☆☆☆

List one choice that was made in the story.

_____

_____

Was this choice wise?      ☐ YES      ☐ NO

Defend your answer with a Bible verse.

" _____

_____

_____

_____ "

_____

# Reading Journal

**Book Title**

_____

_____

_____

**Date:**

_____

**Pages Read Today:**

_____

**Rating**

☆☆☆☆☆

## WORD STUDY

Pick a word you don't know and define it.

_____

_____

Pick a word and write the synonym and antonym.

SYNONYM

ANTONYM

Pick a word and write three words that rhyme with it.

_____

1. _____

2. _____

3. _____

**Book Title**

_____

_____

_____

**Date:**

_____

**Pages Read Today:**

_____

**Rating**

☆☆☆☆☆

## SWITCHAROO

If you could be any character in today's reading who would you be and why?

_____

_____

_____

_____

_____

_____

_____

_____

_____

_____

# Reading Journal

## GET INFORMED

Record in each column as you read.

**Book Title**

_____

_____

_____

**Date:**

_____

**Pages Read Today:**

_____

**Rating**
☆☆☆☆☆

| FACTS | QUESTIONS | RESPONSES |
|-------|-----------|-----------|
|       |           |           |

## THINK ON THESE THINGS

**Book Title**

_____

_____

_____

**Date:**

_____

**Pages Read Today:**

_____

**Rating**
☆☆☆☆☆

In Philippians 4:8, the Bible tells us exactly what kinds of things we should think about. Check off the things below that describe this book.

☐ PURE     ☐ LOVELY     ☐ OF GOOD REPORT

☐ VIRTUOUS     ☐ PRAISE-WORTHY

Tell if you would recommend this book and why.

_____

_____

_____

_____

_____

_____

# Reading Journal

## IMAGINE IT

**Book Title**

_____
_____
_____
_____

**Date:**

_____

**Pages Read Today:**

_____

**Rating**
☆☆☆☆☆

Write a different ending to the story.

_____
_____
_____
_____
_____
_____
_____
_____
_____
_____

## PURPOSE

**Book Title**

_____
_____
_____
_____

**Date:**

_____

**Pages Read Today:**

_____

**Rating**
☆☆☆☆☆

Learn more about the time period of this book, the author, or any topic mentioned. Tell what you found.

**FACT#1**

**FACT#2**

**FACT#3**

**FACT#4**

# Reading Journal

## FAVORITES

Book Title

_____

_____

_____

Date:

_____

Pages Read
Today:

_____

Rating

☆☆☆☆☆

What was your favorite part of the story?

_____
_____
_____
_____
_____
_____
_____
_____
_____
_____

## LEARNING TO DISCERN

Book Title

_____

_____

_____

Date:

_____

Pages Read
Today:

_____

Rating

☆☆☆☆☆

What evidence do you find that shows if the character in this story (or the author) would be a good influence on you?

CLUE #2

CLUE #1

# Reading Journal

## B-M-E

Book Title

_____

_____

_____

_____

Date:

_____

Pages Read Today:

_____

Rating

☆☆☆☆☆

BEGINNING

MIDDLE

ENDING

## INSPIRED

Book Title

_____

_____

_____

_____

Date:

_____

Pages Read Today:

_____

Rating

☆☆☆☆☆

After reading this text, what do you feel inspired to do better?

_____

_____

_____

_____

_____

_____

_____

_____

_____

_____

_____

# Reading Journal

## WORD STUDY

Book Title

_____

_____

_____

_____

Date:

_____

Pages Read
Today:

_____

Rating
☆☆☆☆☆

Write 3 verbs from today's
reading.

1. _____

2. _____

3. _____

Write 3 adjectives from
today's reading.

1. _____

2. _____

3. _____

Write 3 nouns from today's
reading.

1. _____

2. _____

3. _____

## FACT OR FICTION?

Book Title

_____

_____

_____

_____

Date:

_____

Pages Read
Today:

_____

Rating
☆☆☆☆☆

Is this book fact or fiction? Write three clues that help you to know the answer.

Clue#1_____

_____

_____

Clue#2_____

_____

_____

Clue#3_____

_____

_____

The book is ☐ FACT        ☐ FICTION

# Reading Journal

## HAVING COMPASSION

**Book Title**

_____

_____

_____

_____

**Date:**

_____

**Pages Read Today:**

_____

**Rating**

☆☆☆☆☆

Have you ever felt like one of the characters in the story?　☐ YES　☐ NO

Explain your answer. Then draw about it.

_____

_____

_____

_____

_____

_____

_____

_____

_____

## SCENE IT

**Book Title**

_____

_____

_____

_____

**Date:**

_____

**Pages Read Today:**

_____

**Rating**

☆☆☆☆☆

What was the setting? _____

Draw a scene from the book that wasn't in the pictures.

# Reading Journal

**Book Title**

_____

_____

_____

_____

**Date:**

_____

**Pages Read Today:**

_____

**Rating**
☆☆☆☆☆

Write the order of events that happened in the story or chapter.

First, _____

_____

_____

Next, _____

_____

_____

Last, _____

_____

_____

## DARE TO COMPARE

**Book Title**

_____

_____

_____

_____

**Date:**

_____

**Pages Read Today:**

_____

**Rating**
☆☆☆☆☆

Compare yourself with one of the characters.

YOU        BOTH        CHARACTER

# Reading Journal

## SHARE IT

Book Title

_____

_____

_____

Date:

_____

Pages Read
Today:

_____

Rating
☆☆☆☆☆

This book is so _____ that I must tell _____ about it.

Here's why:

_____

_____

_____

_____

_____

_____

_____

_____

_____

## I'M WONDERING

Book Title

_____

_____

_____

Date:

_____

Pages Read
Today:

_____

Rating
☆☆☆☆☆

Question before reading:

Question while reading:

Question after reading:

# Reading Journal

**Book Title**

_____
_____
_____
_____

**Date:**

_____

**Pages Read Today:**

_____

**Rating**
☆☆☆☆☆

## THE BIG IDEA

DETAIL #1

MAIN IDEA

DETAIL #2

## COMPARE IT TO THE BIBLE

Tell about a Bible verse or passage that comes to mind when you read this story.

**Book Title**

_____
_____
_____
_____

**Date:**

_____

**Pages Read Today:**

_____

**Rating**
☆☆☆☆☆